INDEX

Introduction

The Media - Who Are They?	4
Why Get Involved with the Media?	6
So You Think You Have a Story	10
Writing a News (or Press) Release	12
● *Check-list*	*16*
The Reporter Calls	17
● *Check-list*	*19*
Dealing with a Crisis	20
● *Check-list*	*24*
Being Interviewed for Radio	25
● *Check-list*	*29*
Being Interviewed for Television	30
● *Check-list*	*34*
A Press Officer for the Local Church/Association	35
Media Training	37
Reference Section	39
Your Local Media Contacts	40

INTRODUCTION

For many, active public roles, however minor, will often mean some interaction with one form of the media, be it television, radio, or the local press. The church by its very nature is a local organisation. Today more people receive their news from local papers and local radios than they do from the big nationals. Therefore it becomes important for the church to be prepared to interact with the media, particularly on a local basis.

Often, the local minister will find himself needing to respond to an enquiry from a local journalist about a particular event or happening in the town. Others within the church may want to publicise their events and have no idea about how to work most effectively with their local media.

If the media profile of Baptists is to be raised, much of this work must be done through the local church. By their very nature, local Baptist churches will want to arrange and maintain their own links with the media in their own locality. If you listen to the religious programme on your local radio station, how much of the church news comes from the Church of England? This is due partly to the Church of England being the Established church, but partly to the Anglican system of Diocesan Communications Officers who feed the media with their local Diocesan news. As Baptists we need to think about how we will get such information out. If, as Baptists, we want to raise our profile, then we must be prepared to engage seriously with the media.

These Guidelines are designed to help those in churches/Associations and organisations, who may find themselves involved with the media.

The Guidelines can help you in two ways. Firstly, they should remove some of the fear that the very word 'media' can generate within people's minds. Secondly, they can help you to deal more effectively with the media, creating a good impression and enabling you to get your message across.

The Guidelines provide basic information on how to deal with calls from the media, and how to prepare for an interview. They are not designed to help you 'promote' your church. There are a number of books that can do that, and some are listed in the reference section at the back. Some areas of press work are not covered, such as holding a press conference. Such things, dare I suggest, are for the professionals and require a more specialist knowledge.

If you require further information, help or advice, you can always call the Promotion and Communications Office of the Baptist Union of Great Britain - the address, telephone, fax and e-mail numbers are given at the back of this booklet.

THE MEDIA - WHO ARE THEY?

The very word 'media' can be enough to strike dread and fear into the most self-confident person! Yet, for the most part, the media are made up of people just like you and me, who have a job to do, and like many others, bosses to satisfy. Often working under pressure, and to tight deadlines, they will have to be as resourceful as possible to ensure their story is better than anybody else's.

'Media' is of course the plural word of medium, and covers the **press**, (newspapers, magazines, journals), **television** (including cable and satellite) and **radio**.

The glamour star of the three is undoubtedly television! Newspapers, whilst not appearing so glamorous, wield much of the power. When something is written in print it is easy to keep it and refer back to it, whilst television is a more transient thing. The more serious broadsheet newspapers can cover a story in far more depth than television. The front page of a broadsheet newspaper may carry more words than the whole of a twenty minute television news programme.

You may like to spend some time thinking about how the news is constructed on television and in your paper. Next time you watch television news, particularly on ITV, notice how briefly some items are dealt with, and how little information you actually receive. Watch the pictures closely - how do they colour your perception of the story? At least with a newspaper there is more opportunity to read between the lines, taking the story at your pace, rather than being dictated to by a television news editor. How much more information do you glean from reading the newspaper?

Radio tends to be the forgotten medium of the three. Yet, as already pointed out it is a favourite medium, particularly local radio. Radio tends to carry a great deal of news. Of Radio 4's output, for example, almost one-third is news.

It is with local radio that churches are most likely to become involved, perhaps by providing personnel to produce the religious programme, or by providing the news stories and items that will help to fill the air time.

WHY GET INVOLVED WITH THE MEDIA?

In recent years the tabloid sections of the press appear to have taken a perverse delight in exploiting every piece of bad news that comes along. Subsequently our impression of the media is that they are only out to twist, distort, and misrepresent. Naturally we become nervous of being involved.

Such papers are driven by commercial interests, and those that work for them are under pressure to find the stories that will make their paper sell more copies than a rival paper. Often these stories have very little substance.

Yet the tabloid papers are only a small section of the media. Every second of every day there are reporters and journalists working on important and serious stories, often treating them with sympathy and professionalism. Your story could be in this category.

There are three ways in which to become involved with the media:

1. re-active - when something occurs that catches the media's attention and/or imagination and you find yourself, your church, your Association, the central focus of media attention;

2. pro-active - when you have something you think might be worth publicising through the media, a story that they might follow up;

3. getting involved - some churches provide volunteer support for local radio, and in some cases local cable television, to help produce the religious output.

Why be pro-active?

Why not wait for the media to call us? Too often the cry is heard "Why is the church silent on particular issues?" If the church wishes to have a voice in society it needs to recognise the power of the media to give it that voice.

In a society where the media are rapidly expanding there is ever more demand for news and information. Today, the church is no more than a 'bit player' in a much larger drama, and if it wants to have a prominent place in society it must learn to make use of the media in appropriate ways. The evangelist Billy Graham has used satellite technology to preach to more people than would otherwise be possible. Mother Theresa has used the media to promote her image and gain support for the work she does amongst the marginalised of society.

In your local area you might like to use the media to draw attention to your church, perhaps through an event that is happening. You may feel your church has something relevant to offer to the community either in the form of action or in taking a moral stand over an issue.

This should never be taken to extremes. There is no substitute for personal invitations, communication and contact. The media can not do your evangelism for you, but a mention in your local media can raise awareness of your church, or your church event. Unlike advertising a story costs nothing, save the cost of a piece of paper, a telephone call and some time. A story in your local media can also reinforce your personal invitation to an event.

Is there something happening in your church? Is a member of your church doing something a little out of the ordinary? Your local paper or local radio station could be the place to tell your story. Not all your stories need be 'religious'. Does your church have a new building, is it of a special design that may be of interest? Then why not send a release to a magazine about building? Has your church produced particular materials for young people, then why not send a release to a teaching magazine?

All of the magazines published in the UK are listed in several publications which will be available in your local library. *The Media Guide*, *Benn's Media Guide* and *Wildings Press Guide* are just three of the publications available. You may find it worthwhile spending some time in your local library making a note of all your local media outlets. There is a page at the back of this booklet that you can use for this purpose.

Press

Local papers are often small outfits covering large areas and they are desperate for help in getting the news together. A well-written press release about something that is 'newsworthy' could fall like manna from heaven in the lap of an overworked news editor on a local paper. A good story, well-told, can be worth pages of expensive advertising.

Photographs are always useful. They can complement a story and make it more prominent. But always remember the picture needs to tell a story. Try to avoid photographing groups of people meeting in a hall or church. If you were photographing a special event, say for disadvantaged youngsters, a photograph of one or two really enjoying themselves would say far more than a group photograph of a number of youngsters.

Many papers can use colour photographs for reprinting as black and white. To be on the safe side it is best to check with the paper which they prefer.

Whilst you can usually take a colour film in to a high street photographic centre and have your prints returned to you in an hour, black and white photographs will take much longer (usually several days). You may need to go to a specialist in order to have your black and white film developed and printed quickly - unless you have your own dark-room!

Radio

Local radio stations will often be broadcasting for nearly twenty-four hours a day, seven days a week. Whilst independent local radio is predominantly music the last few years have seen the BBC go down the road of speech-based programming. Under new guidelines all BBC local radio stations will have to produce a religious programme.

For many years many BBC stations have been producing religious programmes, often with the local churches providing funding and/or personnel for such programmes.

Do you know who your local religious radio producer/presenter is? Do you supply them with stories? Do you support them with prayer? There are a number of Baptists actively involved in local radio programming. All would be delighted for your support.

If you do not know whether there is a local religious producer in your area then contact Jeff Bonser at the Churches Advisory Council for Local Broadcasting, PO Box 124, Westcliff-on-Sea, Essex, SS0 0QU (tel/fax 01702 348369) who will be happy to supply you with details.

SO YOU THINK YOU HAVE A STORY ...

One of the hardest things to do is to determine what makes a good story. Something may be happening in your church/organisation that you are incredibly excited about. You tell your local paper and they are just not interested. At that point you are ready to give up!

When thinking about what stories you may like to promote look carefully at the kind of story your local media covers. Read your local newspaper. Some newspapers are very small and almost anything will be reported, from school fetes, to holiday clubs, and competition winners. Some local papers cover 'issues', such as homelessness in the area, or the incidence of drug addiction. Listen to your local radio station, what kind of stories are they covering, who are they interviewing? Watch the local news, which will often end with a very small 'filler' item.

It is almost impossible to set down absolute guidelines for what constitutes a 'story' because it will vary from area to area. It is always worth contacting your local media and asking them what type of stories they are looking for. If you feel confident enough you might also like to contact them and offer to make comment on stories involving social, moral and ethical issues.

Generally good stories are always about something out of the ordinary. The usual illustration given is 'it's not a story if a dog bites a minister, but it is a story if a minister bites a dog'!

It may sound cliched, but journalists are always looking for an angle, something that will make a story stand out from the rest. The appointment of a new Association Secretary may not be 'hold the front page' news, but if that same person's hobby happens to be para-gliding, or even tiddlywinks then that could be the 'angle' you need to lift your story from the ordinary to the extraordinary!

WRITING A NEWS (OR PRESS) RELEASE

So you have a story to tell ... but how do you tell it? The best way is to set it out in a news (or press) release. News Release is the preferred term these days as often you will be sending your story to all three media. You may like to telephone the local news editors, explain the story and offer to send them a release. This way when it arrives they will be expecting it.

Writing a news release is always about getting the facts across in a creative and imaginative way that will attract the attention of the news editor/producer reading it.

DO include in the first paragraph the five Ws - Who, What, Why, When, Where

DO remember that a sub-editor will start cutting at the bottom, so get all your important information in the first few paragraphs

DO make sure your release is typed 1.5 or double-line spaced with wide margins, that it is on your headed paper, and clearly says 'News (or Press) Release'

DO think creatively about your opening sentence. This is where you can grab a news editor's attention!

DO try to include a short quote from somebody involved

DO put a contact name and number at the bottom of somebody who will be available to answer any queries

DO try to get your release on to one side of A4

DO give it a simple headline that captures the essence of the story whilst drawing attention to the content

DONT write an essay, or waffle

DON'T write the story, write the facts.

Your release should look something like the example overleaf.

Always be sure of your facts. Never make claims in your release that you are not able to substantiate.

Before sending your release be sure to check the deadlines that the newspaper or radio station is working to. You will need to make sure that your release hits its target at an appropriate moment. Media guides often give the deadlines. You could make a telephone call to the paper. Ask to speak to the news editor, explain that you have a release and ask what time he would like to receive it. Journalists work to tight deadlines and will not appreciate receiving your story after they have decided what is going in to the paper or their radio show.

Date	**FOR IMMEDIATE RELEASE**

HEADING

First paragraph to include the basic information, including the Who, Why, What, When and Where

Second paragraph to expand upon the first paragraph. Further information that you would like included.

Third paragraph to include a quote from somebody involved that will add some human interest to the story, or even an opinion.

Fourth paragraph to include further information that you could live without if it were cut.

ENDS

For further information: Jo Bloggs on 745 1234

Make sure that your release is still relevant. If your new minister is going to be inducted on the Saturday and you have a weekly paper you will need to send advance notice for the previous week's paper, in case they want to cover the story. Then send a release about the event in time for the story to be included in the following week's paper. A week further on and it will be very old news indeed.

You can always send a news release in advance and add the words at the top, in large clear type, 'embargoed until (time and date)'. This has been a much-used device in the past, but sadly many journalists no longer respect embargoes. Therefore it is best to avoid them if you can.

It is always worth telephoning the editor of your local paper, or your local radio producer, to introduce yourself. Ask them what type of stories they are interested in, offer to be as helpful to them as possible, invite them to informal events - cultivating a good relationship can pay dividends in terms of publicity for your church, Association, or organisation.

Finally, remember that the local news editor will probably get hundreds of news releases across his or her desk each week. Unless yours stands out it will end up with many others filed under WPB. But don't despair if your first release achieves nothing - keep on trying! At least you will have registered your church/Association/organisation as one that is keen to work with the media.

See next page for check-list ......

Check-list

- include in the first paragraph the Who, What, Why, When and Where

- type your release in 1.5 line spacing with wide margins on headed paper that clearly says 'News Release'

- keep it to one side of A4 if possible, lists of important information can be attached

- include a quote from somebody involved

- think creatively about your opening sentence

- put a contact name and number at the bottom and make sure that person will be available

- give it a simple but eye-catching headline

- remember that sub-editors start cutting at the bottom

- don't write a story or an essay - write the facts

- a news release is not a *drama* but a *documentary*

- if at first you don't succeed ... keep on trying!

THE REPORTER CALLS ...

Don't panic! There may be two reasons for the call. Firstly, the reporter may be following up on a story that you have generated via a news release. Secondly, he or she may be working on a story and looking for further information or a quote. A story with a 'religious' tone to it may require a comment from a local church.

Before responding in any way ascertain the following:

a) what paper/radio or tv station the reporter is working for

b) if the reporter is freelance, who he or she is expecting to sell the story to, or who commissioned it

c) what the story is about. You may be asked to comment on a local situation, such as a firm closing with subsequent multiple redundancies, in which case you will want to know the whole context of the story before commenting.

If You Are Expecting the Call

- Be prepared to expand on the information in your release courteously and efficiently, even if you are incredibly busy at the time!

- Only give the information that you want to give - don't be bullied into giving any more

If You Are Not Expecting the Call

- Find out what information the reporter is after and offer to ring back in a few minutes. This will give you time to collect your thoughts. But do ring back

- Think about what you want to say. If necessary write some notes out with the salient points

- Take a few moments to relax before returning the call

- Be helpful and polite but don't be drawn into giving more information than you want to by a seemingly friendly journalist - always remember that what you say in the course of a friendly 'conversation' may appear in quotes in the paper the following day

- Never give information 'off the record', this is a device used by experienced journalists and press officers and is best avoided - **if you don't want to see it in print, don't say it!**

It may be that the reporter will want to visit you to interview you. Fix a time that is suitable to you, always remembering that he or she will be working to a deadline. Make sure that you are comfortable, and don't try to squeeze in the interview between other engagements.

Try to create a relaxed environment. Make sure that you will not be interrupted, especially by telephone calls.

If you are going to be interviewed for radio make sure that you are able to go somewhere quiet, unless the interviewer specifically asks for a particular location. (Further information on being interviewed for radio or television appears in later chapters.)

Finally, one day you may receive a telephone call relating to a crisis, whether it be involving your church/organisation, or a major disaster. How to respond to this is contained in the next chapter, 'Dealing with a Crisis'.

Check-list:

- **before answering any questions, find out:**
  - **who the reporter represents**
  - **exactly what the story is**

- **take time to think about what you want to say**

- **make sure you have all the relevant information - don't go public on something you know nothing about**

- **always be helpful and polite. Creating a bad impression could get you the wrong sort of publicity!**

- **never say more than you want to**

- **don't give information 'off the record'**

- **keep calm! Take a few moments to relax before responding**

DEALING WITH A CRISIS

There are two forms of crises; one that directly involves your church, or one that affects your community. Either way how you deal with the media can be very important at this time.

A Crisis in the Church

Sadly, even in churches, things do go wrong. Furthermore when a crisis hits a church it will often make headlines. Being prepared will help you in what can be a difficult and painful time. It is unlikely that any church would have thought about a 'Crisis Management Team' but having such a team in place can be helpful.

The term 'Crisis Management Team' sounds rather formidable. In essence it is usually a team of at least three people: the main communicator/spokesperson for the church; a senior officer of the church (probably the church secretary); and an expert (which may often need to be a lawyer). You may also want to keep your Superintendent informed.

It may be that the spokesperson for the church is the minister. If this is the case then it may be appropriate to invite a deacon or elder to join the team. These three/four people, whilst dealing with the crisis, will be able to offer each other encouragement and support through what could be a difficult time. This avoids one person having to shoulder the burden of a crisis.

The Team should meet as soon as a crisis hits, and preferably before the media know about it, to prepare a strategy. Of course sometimes the media will get there first, and then the Crisis Team will need to meet in emergency session.

Once the news becomes public knowledge the media will be hungry for details. You may get a call from a news agency. These firms make a living from selling stories to the major newspapers so they will often be prepared to go to extreme lengths to get a juicy story to sell. Be wary of dealing with an agency. An agency is likely to approach a member of the congregation for a quote. As soon as possible ask the congregation not to speak to journalists at all but to refer all enquiries to the spokesperson dealing with the crisis.

Never lie, or deny. If something has happened it is better to be honest about it. Try to avoid saying 'no comment' in response to an enquiry. Prepare a statement agreed with the Crisis Management Team, and if the crisis involves the police, have it checked by a lawyer before it is released.

The statement should do the following things:

- give **basic** information
- express **sorrow** for any hurt or unpleasantness
- say what **action** is being taken.

It should never make judgements about the situation or any person involved.

Remember in preparing the statement that what is said affects real people; never say anything that could cause anybody harm or further hurt.

If the police are involved explain in the release that the matter is *sub judice* and therefore it is not possible to make any further comment.

Only offer the statement if journalists approach. Never send it out to all your usual media outlets as you would a news release.

In the midst of dealing with the media it is important also to remember the needs and concerns of all the people involved in the situation. Media pressure can be hard to cope with at the best of times, but even harder when a person is already under stress. Make sure that adequate counselling is available for all parties. It may be that somebody involved in a crisis has the media camped on their doorstep - if necessary be prepared to take the person away somewhere where he or she will be out of the spotlight.

A Crisis in the Community

This can take a variety of forms, eg a local disaster or emergency situation, where the church may be holding the funeral of someone, or even several people, involved. In such situations the feelings of the bereaved must always be of paramount importance. In the case of national disasters the media will naturally be anxious to be involved. The crisis may involve the whole community, such as mass redundancies, or a local dispute.

In the event of funerals in the local church the role of the spokesperson is crucial. They will have to act as a barrier between the media and those involved with, or handling, the crisis. It is their job to keep the media briefed, but also to prevent intrusion into the situation.

Careful liaison will be required over funeral arrangements. Often television companies will share material so it is only necessary to allow one television crew into the church to film. This is done on the understanding that they share their footage with the other companies.

A press briefing should be prepared giving details of the order of service, significant people taking part, and any appropriate information necessary.

In the event of situations involving the community the church may want, or be asked to, make an appropriate statement on the situation, such as an expression of sorrow and the preparedness to act as a support for all involved. In such situations it is important that somebody spends some time preparing a briefing on the situation with as much background detail as possible.

Finally - if you have a crisis situation on your hands then you can always telephone the Baptist Union Promotion and Communications Manager for assistance.

See next page for Check-list ...

Check-list:

In the Church

- have a Crisis Management Team to deal with the situation and to support each other

- avoid, if possible, dealing with news agencies

- ask the congregation not to speak to journalists about the situation

- prepare a brief statement which
  - gives *basic* information
  - expresses *sorrow*
  - says what *action* is being taken

- if the police are involved explain that the matter is *sub judice* and that you are unable to comment

- remember that people involved may be under intense media pressure - be prepared to offer support (and alternative accommodation if necessary)

In the Community

- make sure you know *all* the facts before commenting

- TV companies will share footage of special services

- prepare a briefing for the press with relevant information

BEING INTERVIEWED FOR RADIO

A radio interview may take several forms. It may be done in a studio with a presenter, 'live' or recorded; it may be recorded 'down the line', ie over the telephone; it may be that somebody will visit you and record it in your home, or a chosen location; or it may be that you will have to visit a studio near you and record it in a 'remote control' studio.

Before the Interview ...

- find out what the programme is. If you can, listen in to check out the format

- who else are they inviting on to the programme? What views are they likely to hold?

- make sure you have the facts

- rehearse what you want to say

- write down on little cards the main points you want to get across - but don't script your response, you will sound wooden

- think about the possible audience for the programme and make sure that what you say will be understood by them, in other words, avoid 'jargon' language. Words like salvation, eschatalogical, and transcendent probably will not mean much to your audience. Don't speak over their heads - but don't patronise either.

- remember that you have been asked along because you are the 'expert'!

Practising for a radio interview is not difficult. It only requires a tape recorder and a microphone. Get somebody to interview you and then play it back. How do you sound? How many 'ums' and 'ers' were there? How was your intonation? Get used to the sound of your voice, only when you feel comfortable with how you sound will you interview well.

Warning: some interviewers will talk to you about the conversation you will have before the interview. However, as soon as you go 'live' they will proceed to ask you completely different questions. There is little you can do except be prepared for this to happen! You could of course refuse to answer any questions but with an experienced interviewer you will come off worst and inevitably create a bad impression of yourself.

The trick to answering such questions is to pick up on the **subject** of the question and give the answer you want to give, even if it means not necessarily answering the question. Politicans do this all the time!

The 'Live' Studio Interview

This is likely to be a slightly longer interview, or conversation. You will have more opportunity to get across what you want to say. Don't be put off by all the microphones and buttons - all of those things will be taken care of. Relax and think of it as a discussion with one or two people around your kitchen table.

You will already have thought about the audience and will have formulated what you want to say, so now - forget about them! Just concentrate on the person you are speaking to, maintain eye contact if you can, and have a conversation with him or her. The audience will merely be eavesdropping on that conversation.

For a live interview make sure you know what the first question is going to be and be ready to respond to it.

The Recorded Studio Interview

The atmosphere will be more relaxed but the interview will still be recorded as 'live', so treat it as such. However there will however be opportunity to re-record if you completely mess it up. If you are not happy with anything and would like to re-record say so at the time. Later will be too late.

'Down the Line'

A time will be pre-arranged for the call which the station will make to you. Make sure you are relaxed, and in a quiet and undisturbed location. Have the points you want to make on cards in front of you.

Because of the quality of a down the line interview it is likely to be fairly brief, and because you can not see the person you are speaking to, unless you know and can picture him or her, it is likely to be more impersonal. It is therefore harder to establish a rapport and to feel relaxed. So make sure you get your points across as soon into the interview as possible.

At Home or on Location

The reporter will bring a tape machine, probably either a professional recording version of a personal stereo, or a reel to reel machine. The microphone will only be held about twelve inches away so you will probably sit fairly close together. Don't be intimidated by the microphone. Maintain eye contact and talk directly to the reporter.

The Remote Studio

Some interviews are done in professional studios which you will have to operate yourself, but 'operate' will only mean pressing a button or two. Everything else will be taken care of at the other end.

Again it is hard to establish a rapport with somebody you can not see, and if it is more than a two-way discussion and the others involved are in the studio with the presenter they will have an advantage. So be polite, try to inject as much warmth into your voice as possible, and be firm about having your say.

See next page for Check-list .....

Check-list:

- there are a number of ways you may be interviewed:
    - 'live' in a studio
    - recorded, in a studio
    - down the line
    - at home, or on location
    - in a remote studio

- prepare thoroughly:
    - listen to the programme if it is on regularly
    - find out as much information as you can about what will be expected of you
    - find out who else will be interviewed
    - get your information together
    - ask somebody to interview you and record it as a practice run

- for a 'live' interview always make sure you know what the first question is

- once in the studio, forget the microphone and concentrate on having a conversation with the person interviewing you

BEING INTERVIEWED FOR TELEVISION

On television not only does it matter how you sound but also how you look! With the changing broadcasting scene more and more news is very local. Small news crews are now based across the country collecting information, and filing reports. In some areas local cable channels are now broadcasting with reporters trying to provide a full news service on a very small budget. It may be that your turn will arrive for a local, or even national, television appearance.

We all watch television, but when it comes to being interviewed how many of us would know how to cope? The media are like Christians, they have a language all of their own, which helps to keep the myth, that they are a little bit special, alive and well.

So here is a quick guide to some of the terminology:

Two-shot: when both presenter and interviewee are in the shot at the same time

Close-up: when just your face will appear on screen

Mid-Shot: when your body from the waist/chest upwards will appear on the screen

Noddy: if you watch an interview you will often see a brief clip of the presenter listening to you as you speak - this is known as a 'noddy' and will often be used to cover an edit in the interview.

Cutaways: similar to the above, it will be a shot of something relating to the story that can be used to disguise an edit in the interview

There are several ways in which you might appear on television:

- a 'location' interview at your home/church, indoors or outdoors

- in a studio
    as a guest in your own right
    as part of a panel
    as a 'planted expert' amongst a studio audience in a discussion programme

The Location Interview

The sound will be recorded in one of two ways. Either a small personal microphone will be clipped to your clothes, and the sound man/woman will know the best place to put it; or the sound man/woman will stand with a microphone on a long pole close to you. The microphone is often covered by a fluffy windshield and will be kept just out of the picture.

Even when filming outside there will often be some additional lighting. Usually the light is placed on top of the camera, and it is very bright. You will be asked to look at the reporter who will generally be just to the left or right of the camera, and this should prevent you squinting in the light. Don't look directly at the camera unless you are specifically asked to do so!

Because of the nature of television it is unlikely you will get more than about twenty seconds in which to say your piece. So be prepared. Think what you want to say in advance. Usually the reporter will talk with you about the interview before it begins. Do not be surprised if the interview lasts several minutes but only a few seconds are broadcast.

The 'sound byte' is a common term these days and means a sentence, or two at most, that makes a point and can be easily fitted in to a broadcast piece. Good sound bytes are always popular with newspeople! You might like to think how you can give a brief 'sound byte' answer that encapsulates all that you want to say. This can also avoid your words being cut in the editing suite. Editing can, sometimes by design, sometimes by accident, completely alter the thrust, or meaning, of what you said.

Most news interviews are filmed as quickly as possible and the cameraman/woman may make the decision about where you sit or stand. Try, if you can, to avoid being filmed against a blank white wall, particularly if there is a radiator directly behind you. Such locations are not flattering! No cameraman/woman will enjoy being told where he or she may film you, but if the crew are coming to your church or home you may like to think about the background and politely suggest where you would feel comfortable.

You might also like to think about the subject of the interview. If you have written a report about poverty in your local area, being interviewed in your church study surrounded by computers, telephones and photocopying machines may not give the appropriate signals to reinforce your message!

Although most interviews are filmed quickly, a slightly longer news item may entail the recording of various cutaways (see earlier notes on terminology). These will all take time, so do not plan to 'fit in' an interview between other engagements. You will not do your best if you are worried about time, and neither will you endear yourself to those filming you if you are constantly trying to hurry them up!

The Studio Interview

Be careful what you wear. For a studio interview you should avoid wearing blue. Wear something smart, and make sure you feel comfortable in it.

If you are invited on to a television programme make sure you watch the programme in advance. Who are the presenters? What does the set look like? What is the 'tone' of the programme? Who else is likely to be appearing that day? Make sure that you are fully briefed about your subject. Think about what areas are likely to be covered. If possible get somebody to sit down with you and perform a mock interview. Get them to ask as many difficult questions as they can think of!

If you are part of a panel, find out who else is on it. Do some research into their views. Are they likely to oppose what you say? Usually panels will consist of people who will provide differing opinions - it makes for more interesting television.

Television studio lights are very bright and very hot so always accept the offer of make-up, otherwise you will very quickly look hot and shiny! On the day, take a friend along with you for moral support - the studio will provide hospitality for both of you.

Check-list:

- **appearances are important!**

- **for a 'location' interview think about where it would be appropriate for you to be filmed**

- **unless asked to, *don't* look at the camera, look at the presenter**

- **usually location interviews are recorded very quickly. But sometimes more time is needed so don't plan other engagements around the interview**

- **do your homework**
  - **know the programme content, style and format**
  - **know your facts**
  - **be prepared for difficult questions**

- **know what point you want to get across and think about the most effective way of saying it, briefly (a sound byte)**

- **in a television studio, avoid wearing blue, and never refuse the offer of make-up**

- **be prepared for very bright studio lights**

- **when going to a studio, take a friend for moral support**

A PRESS OFFICER FOR YOUR CHURCH/ASSOCIATION

Many churches and Associations may already have somebody who is designated as their 'press officer'. Sometimes these are people who have considerable media experience, but often they are willing people who have 'volunteered' or been 'volunteered'. How much support are they given? Have they had any training?

Now would be a good time to undertake a communications audit. This sounds complicated but all it really involves is taking a good look at everything you do in terms of communication and asking how effective your publicity machine is!

What is your reason for wanting to communicate? Do you only want publicity for special events? Do you only want to react to an approach from the media, or would you rather be pro-active? Does your church want to become involved in advertising? Who have you appointed to your Crisis Management Team? These are some of the questions you might like to ask.

A job description for a press officer should look like the one overleaf.

The press officer will:

- *gather information about church/Association activities*

- *in consultation with group leaders decide on a publicity strategy for events*

- *identify local press and establish contacts*

- *write press releases, arrange photocalls, and send appropriate information to the local (or even national) press*

- *act as the spokesperson for the church in all media matters*

- *be part of a Crisis Management Team, prepared to respond as appropriate in any 'crisis"situation*

Any Association or church press officer may also find it helpful to liaise with the Promotion and Communications Manager of the Baptist Union of Great Britain.

MEDIA TRAINING

Reading a book is all very well, but there is no substitute for some media training. The opportunity to see the inside of a television or radio studio should not be missed. A day's course on how to write a press release could be of great benefit when you want to use the media to get some publicity for your next major event.

There are many training courses on offer. Some, offered by big companies, can be very expensive. But there are churches that also offer training courses.

Church House Communications Unit - offers training in journalism, being interviewed for radio, radio production techniques, being interviewed for television, and some tailor-made courses. For further information contact:

Canon Andy Radford, Training and Development Officer, Church House, Great Smith Street, London, SW1P 3NZ, tel 0171 222 9011.

Catholic Communications Centre - offers similar courses, sometimes run in conjunction with the Church of England Communications Unit. For further information contact:

Ged Clapson, Catholic Communications Centre, 39 Eccleston Square, London, SW1V 1BX, tel 0171 233 8196.

CTVC - provides high quality training in all areas of the media. For further information contact:

Hillside Studios, Merry Hill Road, Bushey, Watford, WD2 1DR, tel 0181 950 4426

REFERENCE SECTION

Some useful further reading for guidance on how to promote your church:

Keep in Touch Peter Crumpler (Scripture Union Press)

An Introduction to Church Communication Richard Thomas (Lynx Press)

For further help and information:

    The Promotion and Communications Office
    The Baptist Union of Great Britain
    Baptist House
    PO Box 44
    129 Broadway
    Didcot
    Oxfordshire
    OX11 8RT

    Tel: 01235 512077
    Fax: 01235 811537
    E-mail: 100442.1750@compuserve.com

MEDIA CONTACTS IN THE LOCAL AREA

Name	Company	Address	Tel/Fax No